Complexscicity (noun)

Pronunciation: kom-plex--sci- city

Definition: A state of refined harmony where complexity and simplicity converge. It reflects how intricate elements, born from a culmination of completed parts, seamlessly blend to create something that is both deeply sophisticated and universally transparent. Complexscicity celebrates the beauty in how something is assembled—its layers, details, and effort—yet remains accessible and visible to all who engage with it.

Example in a sentence:
"The complexscicity of the sculpture lay in its ability to convey a profound story through a design that appeared effortlessly simple."

Origin: Derived from complexity and a reimagined sense of simplicity, emphasizing the visible craftsmanship behind completeness.

Dedication

This book is dedicated to those who respect the muse—those who understand that creation is not simply an innate gift, but a disciplined art. While it may appear magical to others, those who truly know understand the sleepless nights, countless failures, and unmatched dedication it takes to perfect one's craft. It is for those to whom the muse reveals itself, for those who pour every ounce of their being and passion into their work, that the ability to make magic happens. And for those seeking an outlet to create, this book is for you—a spark, a flare. May it ignite the passion within and light your path toward creation.

This book, "High Vibration: An Alchemist's Guide Through a Classical Renaissance, and Beautiful Complexsicity", represents a collaborative effort blending human creativity with advanced AI technologies. The author extends gratitude to OpenAI's ChatGPT and DALL·E, whose innovative capabilities contributed to the development and visualization of concepts within this work. ChatGPT provided editing for grammar, punctuation, and spell checking, while DALL·E enhanced the book with compelling and illustrative imagery. This partnership between human ingenuity and artificial intelligence exemplifies the future of creative expression.

info@highvibrationsbook.com

TABLE OF CONTENTS:

OVERTURE

- SETTING THE TONE FOR A CLASSICAL RENAISSANCE....... 8-14

FUNGI & THE MUSE:

- THE COMBINATION OF PSILOCYBIN & MUSIC THERAPY FOR A THERAPEUTIC OUTCOME 15-17
- CRAFTING THE MOOD: PSYCHEDELIC MOCK-TAILS IN HARMONY WITH MUSIC......18
- PREPARING PSYCHEDELIC MOCK-TAILS: A GUIDE TO PSILOCYBIN DOSAGE WITH THE TEK METHOD.....19
- MAMA'S CLASSIC LEMON TEK RECIPE......20-21

THE LISTENING EXPERIENCE: WEAVING WORDS AND WONDER

- CREATIVE EXERCISE EXPLORING COLOR AND WRITING BY PROVOKING THE MUSE 25-27
- FULL HIGH VIBRATIONS CLASSICAL RENAISSANCE AND BEAUTIFUL COMPLEXITY PLAYLIST.....28
- ADRIÁN BERENGUER - THE MAN WHO PUTS HATS ON TOP OF HATS.......30-39
- MARI SILJE SAMUELSEN - A SINGULAR VIBRATION AMONGST A SEA OF STRINGS......40-45
- TONY ANN - THE BULL WHO FLOATS LIKE A KITE 46-51
- FLORIAN CHRISTL - THE ALCHEMIST OF MUSICAL NOTES 52-57
- GABRIEL SABAN - MADMAN OF PORTALS, THE DR. STRANGE OF A CLASSICAL RENAISSANCE 58-65
- MATTIA TURZO - THE ROMANTIC THAT RIVALS MICHELANGELO.......66-73
- PAVERS AND MOVERS - MAX RICHTER, TONY ANDERSON, RIOPY, LUDOVICO EINAUDI.....74-83
- TURNING SOUND INTO COLOR - ADULT COLORING SECTION 84-89

FINALÉ: CLOSING ARGUMENTS FOR A CLASSICAL RENAISSANCE

- SETTING YOU ON YOUR PATH TO CREATION AND EXPLORATION 92-93
- ONE FINAL POEM, DUN DITTY DITTY DUN TUN, TUN....94
- SNEAKY PEAKS - SOFT WILD HIGHS 96-100

Coastal ink.

Where words create pictures and pictures create worlds

Forward

Why am I out here screaming from the rooftops, yelling for all to hear? Beethoven, Vivaldi, Chopin—great and ubiquitous as they were—all existed in separate time frames, their music spanning across decades. Vivaldi and Beethoven were separated by 29 years. Although their careers and performances may have brushed against each other in influence, they never truly converged. But today, in the modern era, their works exist in harmony—a convergence unimaginable in their lifetimes.

In this series, we will uncover several composers who are all in the primes of their lives, creating magic and orchestrating some of the most compact and complex melodies. Their music drives our imaginations and emotions to the brink of their fullest potential. This convergence is profound and, quite honestly, so extraordinary that it feels almost unreal. Are we, perhaps, living in a simulation?

As much as I'd love to be the maestro, the pianist, or the classical violinist, my heart is content to be an observer. I am lucky enough to sit in the audience, basking in the vibrations of collective consciousness—witnessing purity, whether in the shared reality we know or some deeper, mysterious non-reality.

This is my attempt to put pen to paper and try to do justice to the magic unfolding in the world today. In times of despair and uncertainty—times of stress and anxiety—there arises a force for good. Like a mushroom sprouting from the decay of a fallen tree, like a flower emerging from the rubble of war, this is the art we need. This is the vibration that can lift us out of treachery and back into the beautiful, breathtaking complexscicity of life.

Overture

There was a time when a renaissance ushered in a new way of thinking, a new way of doing, and a new way of living. Now, if you close your eyes and open your ears, you'll sense that the wheel of time has come full circle. More intricate, more delightful, more inspirational—that time is now.

In this new dawn, there arose a sound—a sound unlike any before, unlike the echoes of past giants: Mozart, Beethoven, Vivaldi, and Chopin. It is an era where impossibility becomes ordinary, where intricate complexities are compressed into the smallest spaces, filling the voids of the canvas. And yet, the picture they create is undeniably transparent, revealing itself for all to see.

If we look back 20 years from now and the names Adrian Berenguer, Florian Christl, and Tony Ann are not etched into our collective consciousness as the brilliance that brought inspiration and understanding to our emotions, we will have lost the battle for our soul. These are the visionaries of our era, the architects of a soundscape that reflects our humanity.

Our society has become so accustomed to punchy lines, crafty lyrics, and generic beats. Of course, there is no shortage of brilliant talent—songs that evoke memories, spark vibrance, and bring joy as we sing and dance along. Yet, therein lies a danger: the danger of provoking the ego, of impressing false images of who we think we are.

When lyrical compositions are played, the words sung to us shape ideas—images of who we are or how we feel. Rock beats can have us jumping and screaming, hip-hop often fills us with a sense of power, as though we could run through a wall. Songs about love bring back memories of past and lost lovers, or better yet, spark the joy of new and inspiring love. These are beautiful experiences that serve a purpose.

But therein lies a subtle danger: the danger of the ego being fed with grandeur that is not authentic to our true selves.

With classical music, we are presented with something different. We sit, we listen, and the melodies—free from lyrical compositions—don't dictate how we should feel. Instead, we simply feel. This is the most authentic expression of our emotions, untethered from external narratives.

When we feel inspired by a classical composition, it isn't because a singer has declared us the "baddest baddie in town." It's because the tones and melodies we hear elevate beauty above all else. They reveal a universal language, profound in its simplicity, one that transcends words and tells no one how to feel—it just is. And in that stillness, in that purity, we find our most genuine selves.

In the intricate melodies of this modern classical renaissance, there is no room to run or hide. Emotions are lifted, soothed, and washed clean. Our default patterns of thought are obliterated into obscurity, leaving us with only the raw, unfiltered truth of who we are.

It is a profound and surreal experience—so authentic, so vibrant—that one cannot help but feel truly alive. For in this music, we rediscover the essence of our being, stripped of pretense and brimming with clarity.

Ages ago, concert halls would overflow with eager audiences, all gathered to witness a miracle of intricate precision, a sublime symphony that left them in shock and awe. These performances would set their hearts ablaze and their minds on paths of profound self-exploration. Yet, it was a privilege reserved for the elite and the fortunate, those lucky enough to experience the transcendence of masters like Chopin and Beethoven.

There is nothing quite like the atmosphere before a grand classical performance. The air hums with anticipation, as if magic itself is coiled in the silence, waiting to emerge. The music about to be performed seems to have always existed—hidden in the patterns of the world, weaving through the unseen lines that connect everything around us. In these moments, it feels as though the melodies have been dancing around us all along, unseen but omnipresent.

Then the first notes break through, and the world transforms. The sounds crash over us, becoming the ultimate reality. Time dissolves, and nothing remains but the raw, unfiltered core of our emotions, laid bare and alive, as the music carries us beyond ourselves into something infinite.

In the modern world, there is space for everyone—no one is left out. The magic of music surrounds us, streaming directly to the little devices we so often demonize as the source of our collective cultural anxiety. Yes, these little "demons" have undeniably spun out of control, overwhelming us with a flood of nonsense and noise. But, like any tool, when wielded wisely, they can unlock something extraordinary. They allow us to tap into the brilliance of song and dance, to cleanse emotional wounds and rediscover ourselves, all from the comfort of home. A good pair of over-the-ear headphones is highly recommended.

In this iteration of High Vibrations, we will explore the magic behind this modern renaissance of classical music. Together, we'll uncover the artists ushering in a new Golden Era, the visionaries blending timeless traditions with innovative flair. We will delve into how this music calms the chaos of the mind, erasing cluttered thoughts to create space for new, transformative patterns to emerge. And, as always, we'll enhance the journey with a touch of alchemy—a magical drink to elevate the experience and take this transformation one step further.

To begin, we must first find a term—one that can help us describe the indescribable sounds we'll encounter through the pages of this book. Brilliance? Yes, the compositions are brilliant, but the term feels too broad. Unbelievable? As Matthew McConaughey rightly said, "Stupidest word in the dictionary. Should never even come out of our mouths—you just saw it, believe it."

Complex? Certainly, these works are intricate. The timing of every element is nothing short of astounding. But here's the paradox: to the ears, it doesn't sound complicated. It feels effortless, natural. Therein lies the challenge—finding a word that blends these seemingly contradictory qualities: intricate yet intuitive, complex yet clear.

If only there were a word that could capture this harmony of opposites. Complex... complexsssii... complexsiciii... EUREKA! Complexscicity!

In a world where music of unprecedented beauty can be created out of thin air, and where paintings materialize with a few word prompts, surely we can conjure new words to capture new experiences. Complexscicity is our attempt to do just that—a term born out of necessity to honor the breathtaking union of sophistication and simplicity.

Complexscicity was born from a desire to grasp the essence of modern compositions—pieces that often feel elusive, defying conventional understanding. To honor their brilliance, we've coined a term that reflects the mastery they embody. These works seem less like creations and more like revelations of universal sounds that have always existed, just beyond the reach of even the most sophisticated composers—until now.

As you explore these compositions, we encourage you to listen freely at first. Let the intricate soundscapes envelop you, immersing yourself in their beauty. Then, listen again—this time, with an ear toward their structure. Notice the countless twists, turns, variations, and instrumental collaborations that unfold, sometimes within a mere two minutes and thirty seconds.

It is in this close examination that the magnitude of what is unfolding becomes clear. These pieces are masterfully woven with such precision and timing that their complexity, though staggering, feels natural and transparent. Together, they form a universal sound experience—profoundly sophisticated, yet accessible to all who are willing to dive in. You haven't a choice now, I've got you (I hope).

Now, let's try to understand how we've reached this pinnacle of both existence and vibrance. To truly appreciate the brilliance of today's classical music renaissance, we must first honor those who lit the way. The luminaries whose visions, struggles, and triumphs have shaped the path to this very moment. These pioneers dared to stretch the boundaries of sound and meaning, crafting works that still resonate deeply within us.

But there's more—beneath the surface of what we hear lies a world of scientific wonder. How does this music reach into the core of our being, stir emotions we didn't know we had, and leave us changed long after the final note? What is it about these compositions that harmonize so powerfully with the human brain? Together, let's embark on this exploration of legacy and science, an intersection where art and neurology collide, illuminating the true power of music.

This interplay between emotion and intellect is no accident. Masterpieces like those of Hans Zimmer and Ludovico Einaudi didn't simply emerge without foundation; they stand on the groundwork laid by extraordinary composers who came before them. These visionaries shaped the sounds we now associate with modern storytelling, helping craft the narratives that leap off the big screen and into our hearts. Zimmer, a name synonymous with cinematic grandeur, has touched the core of human emotion with his scores in films like Interstellar, Superman, and The Lion King. Ludovico Einaudi, the Italian maestro, mirrors this brilliance, not only with his music but with his poetic expressions of life's beauty. His compositions are equal parts meditative and transcendent.

These contemporary luminaries are the pavers of the evolution of modern classical music. They inspire the emerging artists featured in this book—visionaries who add something indefinable yet essential to their work. Perhaps it's one or two elusive elements that elevate their compositions from extraordinary to magical. They create music so profound it suspends thought, leaving only raw, unfiltered emotion.

Classical music, by its very nature, has always had the power to strip away the burdensome thoughts that weigh us down. It soothes the soul, clears the mind, and brings focus to the present moment. As humans, we often avoid the emotions that make us uncomfortable—the ones with daunting allure. Yet, in a healthier society, we would embrace these feelings fully. After all, the only way out is through.

Philosophers and naturalists alike have observed this principle in the animal kingdom. Consider the gazelle: chased by a lion, its survival depends on sheer adrenaline and instinct. But mere minutes after its escape, the gazelle resumes grazing, unburdened by lingering fear or trauma. It lives entirely in the now. Humans, on the other hand, hold onto experiences, reliving and rehashing them to the point of harm. We disengage from traumatic events, trapping the unbearable emotions within us. This, tragically, is the root of conditions like

PTSD. A soldier, shell-shocked on the battlefield, cannot fully release the trauma because the experience is too overwhelming to process.

Though we live in a modern world of abundance—where food, comforts, and opportunities abound—this abundance comes with its own emotional pitfalls. In many ways, the struggles of today pale in comparison to the life-or-death challenges of past centuries. Yet, this comparative ease can create a paradox: we are emotionally unprepared for the nuanced, complex anxieties of modern life. With so many distractions—news cycles that flood our minds, endless streaming options that offer temporary escape—we are less equipped to process our emotions. Remedies like yoga and meditation struggle to penetrate this noise.

Enter the new wave of classical composition—a balm for the modern psyche. This music doesn't merely entertain; it obliterates thought patterns, dismantles anxiety, and brings our emotions to the forefront. With headphones on and eyes closed, these visionary composers guide us on a journey of emotional catharsis. The twists and turns of their melodies massage our emotional spectrum, revealing truths we've hidden beneath the surface. Their music is not just an art form but a lifeline—a force powerful enough to break through the fortresses of distraction and reconnect us with the raw beauty of feeling.

So what is happening in the brain...

Luckily, there is no shortage of studies showcasing the benefits and profound insights into how lyric-free compositions impact our brains and frames of mind. Imagine this: classical music has the unique ability to transport us back to a state akin to the womb. As an embryo, we are immersed in our mother's womb, existing in perhaps the most natural and unburdened state we'll ever experience. There are no thoughts of the outside world, no stress about survival—just an environment where we exist purely in the present moment. This is the transformative power of these compositions, offering a sanctuary where we can shed the weight of thought and anxiety, returning to a state of pure presence and harmony.

Take this study, for example, Janata et al. (2002): the study used functional magnetic resonance imaging (fMRI) to investigate how listening to classical music activates the brain's Default Mode Network (DMN), which is linked to introspection, memory, and emotional processing. Participants listened to familiar and emotionally engaging music while their brain activity was monitored, revealing that music strongly activated areas like the medial prefrontal cortex (mPFC), hippocampus, and amygdala. These regions are associated with autobiographical memory, self-referential thought, and emotion. The study demonstrated that music serves as a powerful cue for memory retrieval and emotional resonance, highlighting its potential therapeutic value for enhancing introspection and emotional well-being.

As chronic illness rises in this country—particularly conditions like major depressive disorder, anxiety, and stress—it has become increasingly apparent that these emotional burdens often underlie physical ailments. In a healthcare system dominated by bureaucracy and corporate interests, many are searching for cures outside its confines. Yet, we live amidst a culture saturated with escapism: endless Netflix binges and comfort foods that do little to heal our deeper wounds. Could the answer to our emotional woes be as simple as art?

The Vartanian & Goel (2004) study reveals that viewing emotionally evocative art activates the insula, a region tied to emotional awareness, and the anterior cingulate cortex, responsible for processing empathy and connection. This research underscores that art isn't just about aesthetics; it is deeply emotional and transformative, engaging neural pathways that help us process complex feelings. By fostering empathy and self-awareness, art serves as a bridge to understanding both ourselves and others, making it a profoundly therapeutic tool for navigating modern life's challenges.

Imagine a book that introduces readers to profound, transformative music, the likes of which we've never heard before, paired with provocative and thoughtful art inspired by these compositions. Picture an immersive experience where every page illuminates your eyes and stirs your soul with vivid imagery, while you learn about each composer—their lives, inspirations, and extraordinary ability to translate emotion into sound with unmatched precision. These are modern-day giants of creativity, and their work exists for us to experience now.

Allow your mind to expand: sit back, throw on your headphones, and let the music resonate through your being. Use an eye mask if you like, and don't forget the powerful imagery you've just witnessed. Let the vibrations of sound and color ripple through your existence, allowing yourself to lay bare your own beautiful complexscicity for the world—and yourself—to embrace. In this space, where art meets music, healing and transformation may begin.

Fungi And the Muse

Now for a quick interlude before we return to the music:

As we progress through this modern renaissance, our culture continues to evolve, gaining a deeper understanding of the world around us. In doing so, we are beginning to reevaluate some of the stigmas that have long confined people to ways of thinking that offer little to no value to society. Before information became widely accessible, governments, corporate interests, and legacy media controlled narratives that shaped how we think about many aspects of life—psychedelic substances being a prime example.

For decades, we have been coerced into a mindset rooted in fear and apprehension. Certain laws and policies hindered meaningful research into substances that could hold incredible therapeutic potential, while the over-prescription of pharmaceuticals became the norm for alleviating stress and anxiety—much of which was exacerbated by legacy media's narrow perspectives. Before the rise of independent media, these outlets were alarmingly effective at implementing their narratives, shaping not only public opinion but also how we think and feel.

We've now reached a tipping point in many areas of society, which is why I believe we are on the verge of an awakening—a true renaissance. Trust in media and government institutions is at an all-time low. With the advent of AI, we can now seek answers to our most pressing questions with unprecedented effectiveness. Many voices are calling for a reimagining of how we approach and treat illnesses that have skyrocketed over the past 20 years, including PTSD, major depressive disorder, and anxiety.

It's striking that these conditions are so prevalent during a time of unparalleled abundance. Yet, despite this abundance, these illnesses dominate our collective consciousness more than ever. Perhaps this renaissance will be the key to unlocking new pathways for healing, not just for individuals but for society as a whole.

One of the major turning points in recent years has been the designation of breakthrough therapy status by the FDA for psilocybin, the compound in magic mushrooms responsible for their psychoactive effects. This designation has opened the door for researchers to better understand psilocybin and its impact on the brain. The clinical data is compelling. However, it is essential to recognize that psychedelics, to achieve therapeutic outcomes, must be treated as tools.

Healing does not come from simply eating mushrooms, sitting on a couch, and watching TV. The process requires intention, preparation, and a conducive environment. When psilocybin comes up in conversation, many people are aware of the remarkable outcomes from clinical trials. Yet, very few understand how these substances are administered in clinical settings. And this is where music plays a critical role—music similar to the compositions we will explore in this book.

These magical performances are profound in their own right. As we've discussed, numerous studies suggest that simply listening to these masterpieces can dissolve negative feelings, relieve stress, and improve cognition. On their own, they have the power to be therapeutic. But when combined with psilocybin—the psychedelic compound found in magic mushrooms—there emerges a synergistic potential for music and mushrooms to foster profound, long-term transformation.

In recent Phase 2 trials conducted by Cybin, a leader in psilocybin therapy research, the results have been nothing short of groundbreaking. 100% of patients suffering from major depressive disorder (MDD) were responsive to the therapy, and an astonishing 80% of participants were in remission 12 months after just two psilocybin dosing sessions. Let that sink in—two five-hour therapy sessions, spaced four weeks apart, paired with psilocybin and music therapy, resulted in 80% of participants no longer meeting the criteria for major depressive disorder.

Let's repeat that again for emphasis: TWO FIVE-HOUR PSILOCYBIN SESSIONS PAIRED WITH MUSIC THERAPY HAD 80% OF PARTICIPANTS IN REMISSION FROM MAJOR DEPRESSIVE DISORDER—A WHOLE FREAKING YEAR LATER! No constant medication, just 10 hours sitting in a chair listening to music!

This isn't just a glimmer of hope—it's a potential revolution in how we approach mental health treatment.

Now a big part of these therapies is the music therapy provided in conjunction with psilocybin. When patients are provided treatment, they are placed in a comfortable set and setting, given an eye mask and a pair of over-ear headphones. They then listen to a choreographed playlist with similar music compositions that you will hear in this book. The profound synergy that occurs between the patient's emotions and music allows a person to feel everything to a level of depth that can illuminate the darkest parts of the soul—an inner journey to understanding that leaves a person grounded in the certainty of their being.

In other versions of the High Vibrations series, we take deep dives into understanding psilocybin and music therapy. But for this edition, we want to focus solely on the profound shift occurring in the classical music genre. For those interested in taking the experience to a new level, more information on psilocybin music therapy can be read about in other editions or on our website, highvibrationsbook.com.

With that said, we could not leave out psilocybin completely. We just had to include a recipe for one of our symphonic-enhancing beverages with a classic lemon tek-infused tea that will warm your heart, give you comfort, and set you up for a profound experience while listening to perhaps the greatest music composers of all time.

Crafting the Mood: Psychedelic Mock-tails in Harmony with Music

The use of psilocybin in conjunction with music therapy has garnered attention for its potential to enhance therapeutic experiences and promote personal insight. When engaging in such a session, it's essential to understand the timing of effects. Psilocybin typically takes some time to exert its influence, with the onset of effects ranging from 40 minutes to an hour and 15 minutes after consumption, often sooner when using the Tek method. This time delay is crucial to keep in mind when planning your session, as it allows for proper synchronization with the music and therapy process.

To maximize the benefits of a psilocybin and music therapy session, the use of headphones and eye masks is strongly recommended. These tools create an immersive environment, isolating the participant from external distractions and helping to channel their focus inward. The combination of auditory stimulation through carefully selected music and the visual seclusion provided by an eye mask can intensify the introspective experience and enhance emotional processing.

A well-curated playlist can profoundly influence the quality of a psilocybin-assisted therapy session, serving as an emotional guide through the journey. The music we provide, accessible via a QR code before your session begins, has been expertly crafted to evoke a wide range of feelings—exploring highs, lows, exuberance, and profound depth. Each song is arranged in a deliberate sequence, designed to support and amplify the therapeutic process. Simply scan the code, hit play, and allow the music to lead you on this transformative path.

Finally, it's profoundly important to consider the concept of "set and setting" when engaging in a psilocybin-assisted therapy session. "Set" refers to the mental state and intentions of the participant, while "setting" pertains to the physical and social environment in which the experience takes place. A positive, safe, and supportive setting, combined with a clear and focused mindset, can significantly influence the outcome of the session, enhancing the therapeutic potential and reducing the likelihood of negative experiences. By carefully considering both set and setting, individuals can create a foundation for a deeply transformative and healing journey.

Preparing Psychedelic Mock-tails: A Guide to Psilocybin Dosage with the Tek Method

If you're looking to elevate your listening experience to new heights, we invite you to follow the recipe on the next page. Using the Lemon Tek method, this preparation harnesses the power of lemon juice to extract psilocybin from the mushrooms, converting it into psilocin, which your body can absorb more efficiently. The onset of effects typically begins around the 25-minute mark, so sip slowly, immerse yourself in the artwork of this book, and let the experience uplift your spirits. This method is an excellent way to create a truly enjoyable and transformative experience.

Always remember to exercise caution and start with lower doses if you are new to psychedelics. Set and setting, as well as having a responsible trip sitter if needed, are crucial for a safe and positive experience. Approach your journey with mindfulness and intention, respecting the potential for profound insights and transformations that psilocybin can offer. Individual sensitivity to psilocybin can vary, so always begin with lower doses if you are unfamiliar with this method or psilocybin in general. Ensure you are in a safe and comfortable environment, and approach these experiences with respect and care.

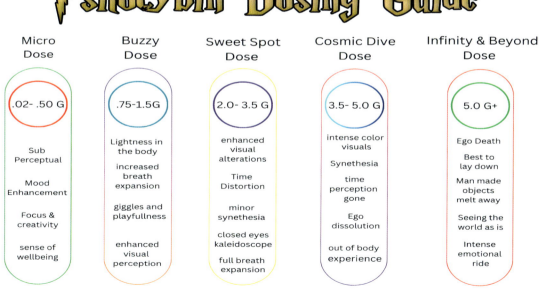

These are only possible effects; individual experiences may vary.

At higher doses, best to be familiar with psilocybin or under the guidance of a licensed practitioner

Ingredients:

Psilocybin mushrooms: Finely ground or chopped (user's choice and dose-dependent).

Lemon juice: 1 ½ lemons, freshly squeezed.

Fresh ginger: 1 ½ teaspoons, grated or pureed.

Honey: 1 teaspoon (optional, for sweetness).

Cinnamon stick: 1 whole stick.

Lemon slice: 1 thin slice, for garnish.

Hot water: 8-10 ounces, not boiling (to preserve the active compounds).

Instructions: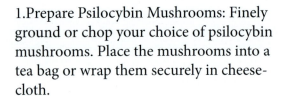

1. Prepare Psilocybin Mushrooms: Finely ground or chop your choice of psilocybin mushrooms. Place the mushrooms into a tea bag or wrap them securely in cheesecloth.

2. Soak in Lemon Juice: Submerge the tea bag in the freshly squeezed lemon juice. Allow it to soak for a minimum of 30 minutes and up to 12 hours to extract the active compounds.

3. Discard the Tea Bag: After soaking, remove and discard the tea bag or cheesecloth containing the mushrooms squeeze and press to etract all of the juice.

4. Add Ginger and Honey: Mix in the fresh ginger (grated or pureed) and honey for flavor and added warmth.

5. Pour in Warm Water: Slowly pour 8-10 ounces of warm water (not boiling—just warm to the touch) into the mixture. Stir gently to combine.

6. Stir with Cinnamon Stick: Use the cinnamon stick as a stirrer, allowing it to infuse subtle, aromatic spice into the drink.

7. Garnish and Serve: Add a slice of lemon to the edge of your cup for garnish, and enjoy the drink mindfully.

🍃🦋🍄 The creation of this magical elixir transforms your psilocybin experience into a mindful ritual, bringing a sense of ceremony and intention to your practice. Infused with the zesty brightness of lemon, the soothing warmth of ginger, and a touch of honeyed sweetness, this drink is both comforting and grounding. As you sip, the gentle heat and aromatic spice relax your body and mind, setting the stage for the journey ahead. Allow its nurturing embrace to guide you into a state of calm and readiness, opening the door to profound insight and connection.

Now back to the music! Let's have some fun! After all, Coastal Inc. is built on the foundation of creating "children's books for adults." We exist to spark imagination, lighten hearts, and ignite intellectual curiosity in our readers. In today's world, with its overwhelming abundance of distractions, it's increasingly difficult to focus on new topics of interest. Sitting down to read a full book becomes a challenge with so much swirling in the mind. Only a few manage to do it consistently.

So we have created this experience book to allow you to disconnect from the world easily and effortlessly. The words should flow off the pages, creating vivid imagery. Don't think—just let the words paint their magic in your mind. Now add in some music, and let your journey begin!

Here's how this works:

Option 1

Simply scan the QR code provided for the full playlist that accompanies this book. It features all the artists we discuss, along with some additional melodies to break up the intensity, helping reset your mind, bring you clarity, and obliterate repetitive thought patterns. Enjoy the imagery in the book, or sit back and close your eyes. This playlist was meticulously curated to ground you, set you on a path of clarity, and unlock new possibilities. Now, add in our classic ginger lemon tek, and buckle up, buttercup—you're in for a majestic ride through the depths of your soul. Should you choose this path, your bravery will be rewarded for weeks, months, or perhaps even years to come.

Option 2

The second part of this listening experience calls for summoning your muse—the creative energy that flows through all of us. Many claim they aren't creative, but that's simply a myth. Creativity takes many forms and flows like a stream. Some streams are larger than others, but I believe everyone has one, even if it's just a trickle.

The muse requires discipline and intention to awaken. The only way to evoke it is to nurture it consistently. I didn't write this book on a whim. I live and breathe my craft. I sit in the chair, put pen to paper, and write—sometimes well, sometimes not so well. The key is making the attempt. You, too, can summon your muse in anything you do, provided you respect it and commit to the time it takes.

Listen to the sounds, close your eyes if you must, or look around the room and take in what you see. Allow these melodies to create images in your mind. Do not think too hard—heck, don't even think at all. Just write down what comes to you. Dance with words, play with them, and love what you feel.

Option 3:

Get the colored pencils out! At the end of the music selections, you will find some beautiful imagery for you to color in. Tap into your creativity with color, let the music block out all your thoughts, and allow your eyes and hands to illuminate the pages. If you can't seem to find the words to create poetry, this option is one that can truly clear the mind. This music will help you stay focused and clear while you paint with the colors brought out by the resounding sounds in your ears.

What to Expect:

This listening exercise is designed to help you evoke your feelings and translate them into words. Scan the code next to each image, listen to the song with a pencil in hand, and let your thoughts flow freely. What comes to mind? Write it down. What does each vibration, each note, and each rhythm say to you?

Allow your emotions to build, and when you write, let their power flow from your core, down your arm, and out through your fingertips. When you give your words power and weight, you release what's inside onto the page. Love what you write because it is a reflection of your emotions. Don't judge it—just let it be. Share it with others if you feel the need, or keep it for yourself; the choice is always yours.

Evoke your dreams in this fantastical scheme, allow emotions to swell, let out a cry, a rebel yell. Feel the fire and passion each of these musical masterpieces represents. Your life is not meant to be bottled up. Through the power of music, we can find our emotional intelligence. We can sharpen our edge or sculpt our intellect into the living, breathing, passionate beings we are all meant to be. Life without passion is dull, like a rounded edge.

Pre-Musical Psychedelic Experience Checklist

Before immersing yourself in a musical journey, it's crucial to ensure that your environment and equipment are optimized for a safe, uninterrupted, and immersive experience. This check list is optimized for a journey with a magical elixr but can also be useful even with out a magic drink in hand!

1. **Charge Devices**: Ensure that all devices you will be using, such as your music player or computer, are fully charged and can last for at least 5 hours without needing a recharge.

2. **Disable Sleep Timer**: If using a computer or music player, disable any sleep timers or screen savers that may interrupt the experience. You don't want your music to suddenly stop mid-journey.

3. **Stable Internet Connection**: If streaming music online, ensure a stable and fast internet connection to prevent interruptions or buffering during your experience or simply download the desieried playlist.

4. **High-Quality Headphones**: Invest in good-quality, preferably noise-canceling, over-ear headphones. Wired headphones are recommended to eliminate any potential complications with Bluetooth connectivity.

5. **Eye Mask**: Consider using an eye mask to eliminate visual distractions and enhance your focus on the music. It can deepen your connection with the auditory experience.

6. **Set Up Your Space**: Prepare the physical space where you intend to embark on your journey before consuming the psychedelic substance. Ensure it's comfortable, safe, and free from potential hazards.

7. **Easy Playback**: Make sure the music you plan to listen to is ready and easily accessible. You should be able to consume the substance, lie down, put on your headphones, and press play without any fuss.

8. **Backup Plan**: Have a backup playlist or source of music in case your primary choice becomes inaccessible for any reason.

9. **Safety Measures**: Inform a trusted friend or family member of your plans and provide them with an emergency contact in case of any unforeseen circumstances.

11. **Comfort Essentials**: Arrange blankets, pillows, or any other comfort items you may need to enhance your physical comfort during the experience.

12. **Mindset and Intention**: Take a moment to set your intentions for the journey. What do you hope to gain or explore through this musical psychedelic experience?

13. **Time Management**: * Clear your schedule and ensure you have no pressing responsibilities. This allows you to enter the experience with a calm, unburdened mind, setting the stage for a more profound and positive journey. Be sure to allow for ample time post journey to integrate your learned experience up to 24 hours :).

By following this checklist, you can create an ideal environment for your musical experience (psychedelic or non psychedelic), minimizing distractions and ensuring that you can fully immerse yourself in the transformative power of music and the psychedelic compounds. Remember to prioritize your safety and well-being throughout the journey.

PLAY LIST #1 FOLLOWS ALL OF THE SONGS IN CHRONILOGICAL ORDER. SCAN AND FOLLOW ALLONG WITH THE POETRY

PLAYLIST #2 IS SPECIFICALLY DESIGNED TO BE ENJOYED WITH MAMA'S CLASSIC LEMON TEK. DO NOT SHUFFLE; START FROM THE BEGINNING, PUT ON THE EYE MASK, AND GET READY FOR A TRANSFORMATION.

ADRIÁN BERENGUER

This man's virtuoso artistic ability is almost unfathomable. He crafts his compositions with the intensity of Van Gogh but with the edge of Banksy—a charismatic madman painting vividly intricate murals. His brilliance, as if he were a casual artist decorating the brick walls outside city hall, his genius hiding in plain sight.

The keys lie in the strings, but it's everything beyond them that defines the magic. Bursting through walls is where the true beauty lies—this man can play flutes within the strings. His notes tap gently on the eardrums, creating friction, ecstasy, a fuzzy sensation like the static that raises your hair after a slide in the playground.

To listen to his compositions is a journey to childhood freedom. The neighborhood playground becomes his canvas. Take a step inside, hear the music, and jump on the carousel—it's a ride you'll never want to end.

All these artists seem to tap into some miraculous stream from the unknown, but Adrian is the true magician. His compositions are like pulling a rabbit from a hat, a rose from his sleeve, or a nickel from behind your ear—effortless yet mesmerizing. The sense of wonder he creates is unparalleled. Like saturated streams of color splashed against a wall, you might anticipate chaos. But when the veil is lifted, the master painter is revealed, leaving all who bear witness in shock and awe.

No wonder he is the artist he is, his roots and his soul are based in brass. He began his music career learning the saxophone, an intriguing start for someone playing the compositions he is currently. Perhaps this is where he learned to slide and bend to weave the beautiful soundscapes with soulful intent. The image of a man playing the saxophone, with a bouquet of roses sprouting from the horn—vivid, and romantic—would be a perfect depiction of the depth and passion he brings to his craft.

This crafty Spaniard continues to produce some of the most astounding soundscapes we've ever heard. Almost surreal, which is probably why his music has been featured in numerous video games. His decadence is perfect for the alternate reality world that captures the imagination of so many. The compositions he writes add detail to every storyline within the game. When listening to his music, it is almost as if he paints a virtual world on top of reality. The real suddenly becomes surreal, a hat on top of a hat.

Red Dress

The swift knife cuts at you
like the slit that rides up the leg.

As you get to the seam,
a thunderous chant halts you
before you rip the precision cut
into a Frey of tattered fabric,
like the mistress who walks down
the spiral staircase, waiting for you.

As you hold roses in hand,
she walks past you without a hint of care.

Head to shoulder,
a silent whisper to come near,
hands to shoulder, breath to ear,
more than a tingle—a tremble.

There is depth in all that is fair.

Aware

Playful bounce wanders in its ambivalence,
quick turns slip through rounded edges.

Steps glide into a delicate waltz,
then picks up into a measured sprint
toward the cliff's edge, arms out wide.

A sea mist from the crash of a wave below
permeates the air,
the cool salt mist refreshing and aware.

Nearby,
a hillside of daisies bending and twirling,
a surrealism in their dance.

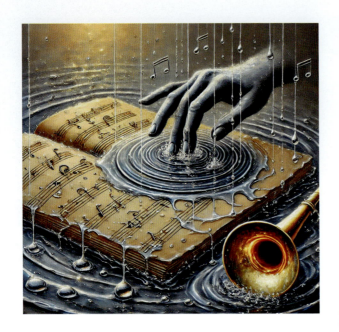

Baby

Fingertaps on the pad
2 then 1
slight pitterpats,
we fade into gentle slaps,
raindrops drip drap
the puddle claps back
reverberating tracks,
slight overlaps.

Streets

This life we go round,
Upside down the merry we go round.
Skipping so insightful,
My, this play of life so delightful.
Bops and weaves,
Flutes like kites above the trees.
Merry and free,
This is the life for me.

Life

Sails a flap,
the white crest of waves far as the eyes can see,
each convergence a subtle crash,
to the great wide open we're out to sea.

As night sets in,
stary eyed Jack sings to me,
his flutes from the crow's nest
dance across glimmering seas.

This journey we will see.

New Way

A DELICATE TAP EMBRACES YOU,
AN OLD FRIEND, A JOURNEY AHEAD,
AN UNCHARTED PATH.

IN THE DIM BLUE HUE OF NIGHT,
WITH EACH STEP THE MAGIC UNFOLDS,
FIREFLIES IN THE NIGHT.

EYES PEER THROUGH THE JUNGLE,
THE ENCHANTMENT SURROUNDS YOU,

GUIDING YOU,
A NEW LIGHT, A NEW LIFE.

Deer

Hunting in a cosmic scene,
Prowling through the galactic gleam.
Stars and blue beams
the lumberjack springs,
leaping across Saturn's rings.

Pipes and fluty things,
These strings and all of the things.
A madman, passion, and all of the things.

Presto

Without a second to fear,
The magic black cat with arched back appears.
Jesters and magic acts,
The candy-colored carnival land appears.

Tightrope acts and flapjacks,
Bearded ladies and crackerjacks.
Enter the striped tenant and never come back—
A lion tamer and slinky acrobats, all in the same act.

A carousel spins under moonlight's gaze,
Where time is lost in this carnival's haze.

Mari Silje Samuelsen

Amid a sea of strings, a singular vibration emerges, cutting through like a gust of wind slicing a gentle breeze. A tender veil envelops you—a shiver, an awakening. She wields her artistry like a Rembrandt, fierce yet tempered by a beauty that commands the spotlight. Around her, the supporting sounds rise like mycelium spreading through the earth, intertwining at her feet and lifting her high for all to see. She is majesty.

Fierce beauty defines her, both inside and out. She wields her bow like a warrior defending all that is light and golden. Each stroke is deliberate, focused, and precise—a beam of vibration piercing the night, banishing vile thoughts and summoning strength. Her music sharpens the senses; your pupils contract, your gaze locks, and with unerring precision, you strike. This is the transformative power Mari Samuelson imparts to every one of us as she stands on stage, radiant in her glory. She commands your attention, making it impossible to look away—and why would you?

Mari Samuelsen's playing is otherworldly—I am convinced. Or perhaps it is of this world, and she simply makes the unimaginable possible. This Norwegian prodigy began her musical journey at the age of three and, by four, was under the supervision of renowned violinist Arve Tellefsen. She has performed across the globe, gracing stages such as New York's Carnegie Hall, Paris's Philharmonie, and Berlin's Konzerthaus. To see her perform live would undoubtedly be one of the greatest experiences of your life—her violin, the one set of strings that can neither be compared to nor drowned out by any other.

Mari has collaborated with luminaries like Max Richter, Jeff Mills, and Dubfire. Her dedication to her craft elevates masterpieces by these profound composers to an entirely new dimension. When she plays, the music transcends. Pieces that are stunning when performed by a full orchestra become pure enchantment in her hands. It is as though a golden orb encapsulates the orchestra, lifting and illuminating everything in its light. As the music swells, Mari herself seems to rise—suspended, playing, and twirling silk tapestries of sound.

November

THE GENTLE SING OF THIS EFFERVESCENT DREAM
LULLS YOU INTO A PEACEFUL STREAM.
AMIDST THIS IDYLLIC SCENE, A BEAUTY QUEEN QUITE UNSEEN,
THE ROSE THAT ARISES FROM A TUMBLE OF THORNS.
CLOSE YOUR EYES, THE LIGHT FROM THE STAR
IGNITES LIKE A BURNT ORANGE AUTUM FLAME.
BEHIND THE VEIL, EYES WIDE SHUT,
THIS VIBRATION ERASES ALL OF THE PAIN.
THROUGH GENTLE HUMS, THE HEART TAKES FLIGHT,
CHASING THE ECHOES OF ETERNAL NIGHT.

 Must Watch!

Time Lapse

Shadows like to dance,
An intricate play, light and dance.
The floor, one half glows,
As darkness grows.

The shadows on the floor,
Moving ever slow,
Delicate in their advance,
Light to darkness—this is their dance.

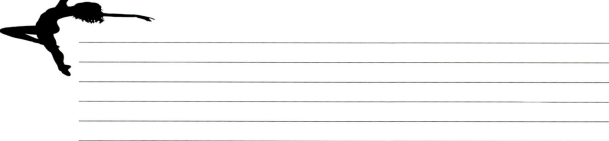

White Flowers Take Their Bath

Hummingbirds in the night, fireflies the eyes delight.
Cherry trees and honey bees a sweet escape on a moonlit breeze
Beautiful colors the autumn leaves
Silent sorrow in the dark of night, as lovers grow
The night hums softly cloaked in white.

Glass

Swift and simple, the bobcats punch and play,
The interplay between all things dance,
Connected by this ambient trance.
Back and forth, they tumble,
Swift and simple, an effortless dance.

44

TONY ANN

He pings the notes of existence with sheer fluidity, an interplay that touches both the highs and the lows in the same instant—a light ping announced by a thunderous bang. A bull performing a tightrope act in a china shop; the Sagittarian drifts like a kite in the sky, etching the canvas with streaks of liquefied colors. The piano sings without a hint of space between notes, as if a violin virtuoso never lifts the bow from the strings, each sound flowing—the harp of piano strings.

An immaculate craft this man creates—a dance across the universe. Perhaps the greatest piano player to ever play. At times, he transforms keys into strings, melodies into journeys, and feelings into sound. As if you can taste colors, you can hear the universe sing when this man plays his piano strings.

Each song pulsates through you, touching every corner of your existence. A prodigy nonetheless, this man—a mere 30 years old—plays as if a lifetime has passed him by. How he hears these melodies is as if he were a man withered by the weight of life, nearing its end—a life of experience behind him, happy and content, no more regrets, only time to peacefully reflect, to listen to the music and smell the roses. This, however, is a young man whose emotional brilliance flows into existence from his core, through his fingertips, and onto the keys—a play unfolding for all to witness.

Tony Ann, a Canadian-born piano prodigy, found his way to Berklee College of Music to hone his talents. He has collaborated with the likes of The Chainsmokers—an expected collaboration for a youthful prodigy playing alongside a group that attracts ears which would naturally flock to his solo aspirations.

With so many years ahead of him to create and flourish, it's impossible to imagine what he will bring into existence. It seems as though one day, he might just sit at the piano and, through his ability to touch the keys no one else can see, transform it into some otherworldly instrument from another dimension.

The bull who floats like a kite, his pronounced playing ability is followed up by the lightest of touches. He floats across the keys while encompassing the power of a raging bull. Each emotion is played out through his fingertips.

RAIN

The tick of a clock resonates
In harmony with the space around us.
As you close your eyes,
The endless ticking becomes part of existence—
No time, only wonder.

Brilliance, speed, tenacity, and patience
All converge into a singularity—
Fierce yet calming.

It is as if a ballerina, draped in silk,
Twirls in the darkness, into the depths.
In the darkness lies confidence—
No thoughts, just movement.

Time

Spectacular things weave a dreamy spin,
Time will not end.
A wizard's wand in the painter's hand,
The harp of the master piano man.

The space between the butterflies' dance,
A flutter, a spin, up and up,
Like two kites in the wind.

Streams of glitter and gold unfold,
Nothing like the story that was never told.

Lost

Right, then left, right, then left,
The pen taps, the paint splash.
Ideas bloom, then drift away,
Lost in this triptych phase.

An illuminating haze,
The mind bends and turns,
Lost in this beautiful craze.

Wonder

Echoes bounce off the light,
A near impossible feel.
An invisible field, full of all things real.

Belief the only way to touch
This near invisible field.
A silk screen dances unseen,
Between you and me.

A quiet force, tender and still,
Awakens us to this enigmatic feel.

Florian Christl

The fuzzy friction between lovers' legs, the humming of the wind across the sands, a gentle crash.

Florian Christl entraps you in the journey you were always meant to take. There is no depth his scores cannot reach; they lift you from the pits of the deepest despair and propel you forward, like the slingshot of a shooting star. Each section feels almost distinctly different from the last, yet the same melody weaves through it all, like the subconscious — always there, always present.

The German composer Florian Christl, born in 1990, began his music studies at the age of six. Like the greats across time, much of his education is self-taught, a testament to his innate connection to the art. The magic that flows through his consciousness is undeniable, an unyielding force that commands attention. The greatest painters, musicians, and writers often share similar origins: their talent is not something learned in school but an intrinsic gift they embrace and live.

For Florian, there is no choice but to create and expand. Without this outlet, one might imagine his life descending into chaos and debauchery, for his muse is relentless. It is his diligence and reverence for this muse that allows him to rise above, crafting some of the most brilliantly articulate narratives through the universal language of lyric-less compositions. His music is not merely heard — it is felt, a profound storytelling that transcends words.

As we have previously stated, there are masters — both past and present — who have paved the way for the evolution of this modern-day Renaissance in classical music. Along with Beethoven, Florian cites the works of Ludovico Einaudi and Max Richter as some of his inspirations. Reverence and gratitude are a must if one is allowed to touch the invisible fields that flow all around us and bring them out for all to hear.

The alchemist of musical notes, the artist with the brushstroke that paints a dream in a single sweep — this is Florian Christl. He is the kind of person you leave alone for a few minutes, and upon your return, he's created the universe with just a few simple elements. This is his gift. Listening to his arrangements allows you to envision a journey that has you accomplishing all of your wildest dreams. Then, take off the headphones, keep his melodies in mind, and go out and accomplish all of those dreams.

Close your Eyes

The Irish hillside abounds,
Wired grass elegant in the wind.
The life filled muse abound
Twirls and spins.

The violins churn into the mix,
Blending the delightful pings.
This journey won't soon end.

A new melody flys in,
A dragon fly dances,
A fox settles in,
A long night,
A breath of air,
Close your eyes,
It's time your life begins.

Is This Now

A tale meant to be told,
Marks of strife unfold,
This is how glory is told.

The artisan man has always had a plan,
Hand over hand, each shot has been planned.
No one should ever doubt the artisan man,
For even though things do not always go to plan,
Magic lies in the artisan's hands.

Bulgaria

Tragic steps that lead to magic steps
Those first leaps after a tragic inner death
tippy toes then skipping stones
New flowers grow a new life unfolds

Leidenschaft

Life is but a series of particle beams
Each toe taps a different note.
Straddle two lines—ting ting,
Hop five at a time—bing bang.
Jump, spin, and float,
Make sure to hit each and every note.

GABRIEL SABAN

This madman of time portals is the Dr. Strange of the classical renaissance. A matador—calm and brave—his cape that lures the bull is a bow, creating a portal to another realm.

The escalation into ecstasy reaches a crescendo, where the immersion of strings seamlessly blends with the thunderous crash of each drop. Speed fuels the relentless ferocity, with no goal in sight—only the frantic intensity of the moment. It is where flow meets execution, where the boundaries of time and space dissolve into something profoundly vivid. Only those who leap in with both feet can dip into the portals that send the mind into a tizzy of imaginative dreamscapes.

Each composition creates a Dalí-esque scene, conjuring the most surreal and vivid imagery when experienced. These compositions don't simply complement the visual narratives of cinema—they dictate them. They write the movie scenes instead of allowing the movie scenes to dictate the sound experience we hear on the big screen.

Much like Dr. Strange, who donned a lab coat before his time-warping cape, Gabriel crafts his masterpieces in a laboratory akin to the high-tech lairs you'd expect to see in superhero movies. His compositions are engineered with the most advanced technology in music today. Perhaps he's even warped into the future, pulling otherworldly instruments into his lair to create these mind-altering music pieces.

A master composer, classically trained in piano and clarinet, who ventured into the field of sound engineering—this is absolutely the backstory of a mastermind akin to Dr. Strange if ever there was one. His pieces have appeared in iconic films such as *Oppenheimer*, *Frozen II*, and *Avengers: Endgame*.

His music doesn't merely accompany scenes—it transforms them. It creates such vivid imagery that listeners are transported into worlds of their own making, where imagination takes flight, and reality bends to the will of sound.

Golden Cage

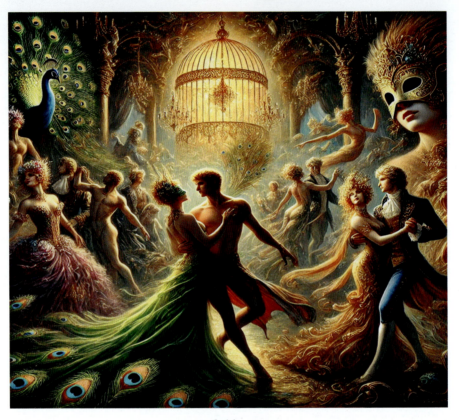

Fanciful beams,
The birdcage of all your wildest dreams.
A masquerade into one another's dreams,
Pirates and fanciful men,
A peacock's tail—this masquerade is one to attend.

Gowns and half-naked men,
This waltz is one you'd never want to end.
A golden cage—
Only way out is to attend.

Dark Acadamia

The dominant, the submissive,
Whips and chains, candlelit flames.
A game that demands to be tamed,
How do we maintain?

A dance down brick-laid lanes,
Distinguished men and elegant dames.
Clashes and fantastic bashes,
This path will lead to ashes.

Touch The Sky

Planks in the sky—two swordfighters locked in battle,
Leaping from beam to beam, through staircases and doorways,
A Dalian dream.

Climbing or falling, each step, each beam,
Each door a path to some in-between.

The battle rages back and forth, up and down—
Reach too far or hesitate too much,
And with one woeful step,
You'll find yourself lost
In the shimmering haze of this boundless dream.

Creative Minds

Digital chess
In the three-dimensional world—
The knights, the bishops, the queen,
A marvelous dance.

Back and forth they go,
Striking each and every blow.
Craft and witty intent,
The queen's masterful plan,
A sacrificial lamb.

A bend and a blow,
Oh no—
A dagger out from under
Sir Bishop's cloak.

No time to see,
The fateful queen,
Too caught up
In the in-between.

MATTIA TURZO :

The Sculptor in his garden, the rays of light, each curve each bend elevates a new sensation. Soft hands mold the clay into the finest poetry of the Italian Renaissance. In this utopian scene, the vibration of the unseen emerges into your wildest dreams. A charge and a jolt as chaos unfolds, this Renaissance man stricken with a madness full of compassion and play.

Mattia Turzo, the fiercest of composers, filled with fire and brimstone, possesses an elegance draped in passionate scores that send your mind sprinting through the dark of night, set to conquer all things love and fear.

The mighty Italian is as bold as any; his intensity is provocative. He can plunge you into the depths of your rage, and in the very next instant, present an arrangement of the most eloquent artistry that leaves you in mystified awe. This is emotional brilliance—capturing the entire spectrum of human experience, allowing you to see everything you are, all within the most immersive soundscapes that strike you in every feeling.

Turzo embodies a Romanticism that rivals that of the renowned Italian artist Michelangelo. Each of his works is intricately carved, like marble masterpieces—perfectly balanced and shaped. His sounds elevate every emotion, just as it is utterly breathtaking to view the Pietà in person. The marble is so masterfully crafted, fitting the mind so seamlessly, that there are no questions left to ask; all you can do is marvel at what stands before you.

This is Mattia Turzo.

His works have been performed in concert halls across Italy and around the globe, with many of his compositions featured in movies and video games. This maestro masterfully blends the most sophisticated classical elements, passed down through centuries, with modern techniques and cutting-edge technology, heralding a contemporary classical renaissance.

Like the finest artisans, his ability to weave countless intricate elements into cohesive compositions is akin to the craftsmanship of a master carpenter or the artistry of history's most celebrated sculptors. This is your introduction to the Michelangelo of our time.

Prateria

Choo choo trains and propeller planes
Dancing high where freedom reigns.
Comets ablaze, what is this life full of rage,
A fiery heart - set the stage.

Walk this path, eyes ablaze,
Conquer this rage.
Play in the clouds with the sun aglow,
Through the fire, a truth remains:
Find the beauty in all the rage.

Floris Folium

The matador's notes set the gunpowder line ablaze,
The fire makes its way through a wandering maze.
Mystery leads us in all this craze,
Gunpowder lines ablaze.

Drum beats bang in this never-ending maze,
The big hand on the watchtower clock ticks and tocks.
It's time to set this life ablaze.

Forefathers

The ballroom floor, chandeliers like gems,
A gentleman, a yellow gown.
Chivalry stirs, on the mend,
Hand to back, a servant's bend.

He twirls her with confidence, of a 1,000 men
Hues of blue, swirls of yellow blend,
A beginning marked by a story without end .

The Sublime

Dominance with confidence lifts
Into measured playfulness,
Striking at each beat,
The marble begins to chisel away.

A deafening madness at play,
Reverence with a subtle fade.
The madman, the sculptor, the writer,
A Renaissance man at play.

Max Richter, Tony Anderson, RIOPY, Ludovico Einaudi:

Amongst this acrylic ceiling of masters, poets, and modern-day Da Vincis is a group of pavers and movers, and those who are also dreaming amongst the stars, sprightly in delight, finding moves and dashes that spring across the emotional wellspring we all tap into. Playing every note to touch each and every moat.

From the forefathers to the young dash-hounds, this listening experience is meant to illuminate the mind as if looking up at the ceiling of the Sistine Chapel for the first time, hues of blues so perfect they create a glimmer of hope and a spark in the eye. Take it all in and expand your mind. From Einaudi, who's as vivid as a rose and sharp like the tip of a thorn, to Richter, who will run a bow across your arm that creates so much fuzzy friction you'll become an electric beam in the in-between. Mix in some vim and vigor of youthful talent, and you'll be sipping the finest wines, basking in the sunshine of the Spanish countryside. This is your glimmering white light of serenity. Deep breaths, close your eyes, and see the light.

As you spring across this lively realism of a dream, understand that all around you is beauty: blue crashing waves, lockets upon a fence, a dash of bitters to illuminate the senses. Listen while you dream, and awaken to this vivacious pattern of arrangement we call life. The music becomes the brushstroke, painting moments you've longed for yet never known. Each note, each pause, stretches time into eternity, leaving a trail of stardust in its wake. It's an invitation—a beckoning to step beyond the frame, where the colors of sound blend with the hues of feeling, shaping an infinite masterpiece that only your soul can fully perceive.

King

Shore line hits the wind
Unleashes the king within
The white wash wave cleanses the sin within
Shorelines and skylines the art within.

Tony Anderson

Sorrows and depth swirl within this dream,
Dire consequences hanging in the balance—just one missed step.
In a moment of time, the ballerina slips;
Her fall is elegant, folding seamlessly into a sitting pirouette.
On the ground, head bowed, as if this was always how it was meant to end.
A beautiful scheme in this lavish dream.

The Quality of Mercy

Max Richter

Ethereal

Repetitive drift, dripped in decadence,
The scale slides like the drop of rain
Down the stem, but no savioring in sight—
An endless twirl, slow motion again and again.

The sorrow of love, the suspended thought,
Calmness brings confidence,
But the twirl never ends.

Txmy

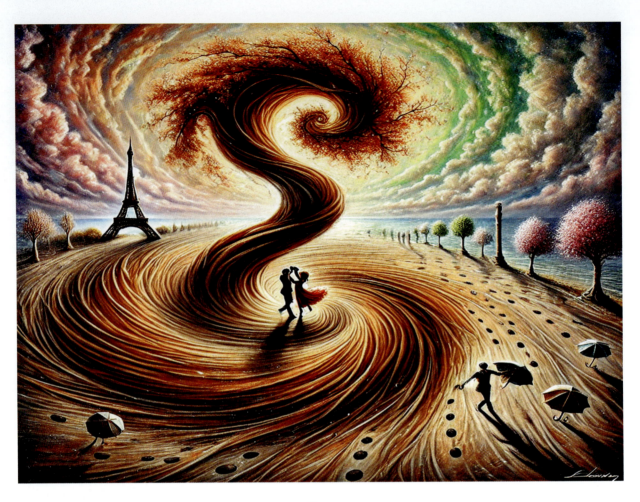

A Tale In Paris

Lines, a vibrating vine,
The swirl of the knot in the oak divine.
Brown silk, a shimmering shine,
Dotted paths where worlds align.
The sing of the sea
Umbrellas stretch as far as the eyes can see.
Under skies of dreams, where hearts run free,
Dancing in Paris, beneath the Champs-Élysées tree.

 RIOPY

Experience

The spectrum of a rainbow glares across the glass,
Stepping across each color, the journey begins.
The beat picks up a determination within,
The patterns on the walls blend in.

You slowly realize—
In the stillness, it comes:
Every color, every step,
flighting across these hazy lays.
it was always meant to be the greatest days.

Ludovico Einaudi

Finalé

If there isn't a classical renaissance already underway, then let's spark one! Emotions are the key element to living a healthy life. Keeping our emotions well-balanced and freely flowing, while also understanding them, is the ticket to self-discipline and peace of mind. The frantic man is often agitated, usually pent up from suppressing his emotions for the sake of "being a man." The sorrowful woman is one who hasn't found a proper release mechanism to let her inner wellspring heal.

Through powerful emotional compositions and creative exercises, we can all regulate the flow of our emotional stream to a steady, consistent rhythm—neither overwhelming and flooding nor trickling and stuck. Being emotionally well-balanced allows us to fully embrace life in the present moment. Too much anxiety, and we worry about every detail; too much detachment, and we miss the finer points of life.

Through this experience, we hope that you were able to hear the beautiful "complexscicity" that these musical poets convey in their art. Life itself is a beautiful complexsicity—it seems so wild and unpredictable, yet it can also be as simple as sitting down with peace of mind, taking in all that the world has to offer. This duality mirrors the music you've just experienced: intricate and profound, yet effortlessly accessible in its beauty. These compositions are not just songs; they are emotional roadmaps, guiding us through the chaos and clarity of existence.

With the growing advancements in psychedelics and the revival of more holistic approaches, we stand at the cusp of a paradigm shift. Imagine a future where music, nature, and self-expression replace the reliance on pharmaceuticals and medications that often mask our pain instead of healing its source. Psychedelics, paired with intentional creativity and introspection, have the potential to unlock doors within our minds, helping us process trauma, dissolve outdated mental patterns, and awaken to the vast potential of our emotional and spiritual selves. When combined with the therapeutic power of music and the grounding force of nature, they offer a pathway to wholeness that feels both ancient and new.

By returning to these natural and creative modalities, we can nurture not just our bodies but our souls. The rustle of leaves, the rhythm of waves, the soaring crescendo of a symphony—these are medicines we've always had at our disposal. They remind us of our place within a greater ecosystem, one that thrives not on pills but on connection and understanding. When we step outside to breathe in the fresh air and listen to the symphony of life, we begin to heal in ways that transcend the physical.

Finding time to escape into our inner worlds through the power of music, paired with creative exercises, helps our minds cut through the noise of the outer world. This process allows us to be fully ourselves within our own minds. When we remove the headphones and feel proud of our creative expressions, we become more present, aware, grateful, and ready to face the world in front of us—through rose-colored lenses.

We all advance through this time together; this is a collective consciousness, all walking and roaming this earth miraculously in this moment. With so much strife and despair, but also so much overwhelming abundance, it can be difficult to truly appreciate the beauty this world has to offer. These emotionally evocative pieces, so profound in their impact, can help us reconnect.

Music is one of the few universal languages we all understand. It speaks to the heart and bypasses the barriers of culture, language, and personal experience. When we immerse ourselves in a beautiful composition, we are not just listening; we are participating in an emotional dialogue with the artist, who poured their soul into their work. This connection reminds us that we are never truly alone in our struggles, nor in our joys.

Creative exercises like journaling, painting, or dancing add another layer to this journey. When paired with music, they become tools for self-expression that tap into the subconscious. We may discover truths about ourselves that have been buried under layers of routine, stress, and societal expectation. These moments of revelation are deeply healing, enabling us to better navigate our internal and external worlds.

Imagine a world where people pause to create, to feel, and to connect with themselves through art and music. This is not an unattainable dream; it is a choice—a practice we can incorporate into our daily lives. By doing so, we elevate not only our individual well-being but also the collective vibration of our communities.

As we allow ourselves to feel more deeply, we also begin to see the interconnectedness of all things. This recognition of unity fosters empathy, compassion, and understanding, qualities that our world so desperately needs. Through the simple yet profound act of embracing music and creativity, we can contribute to a ripple effect that touches others in ways we may never fully see.

So let us step boldly into this renaissance, one note and one stroke at a time. Let us honor the emotions that make us human and channel them into art that transcends time and space. If the world feels heavy, let music lighten the load; if it feels chaotic, let creativity bring clarity. Together, we can rediscover the beauty and harmony that have always been within us, waiting to be uncovered.

The classical renaissance is here for the taking. Will you join in the symphony?

Dun ditty ditty dun tun, tun,
Dun ditty dun tun tun.
A step, a slide, a slithering snare,
Apple pie—oh, fencers beware!

Dun ditty ditty dun tun tun,
"On Guard," whispers near,
Dun ditty dun tun tun,
Will you, my dear?

Da ditty da dun, tun, answers appear,
Decadence I see; decadence is here.
Dun ditty dun tun tun,
No flight, no fear, just a dance sincere,
Da ditty da dun, tun, the path is clear.

A rhythm, a riddle, a spiral to be,
Decadence is you, decadence is me.
Dun ditty ditty dun tun,
Excuse me, dear—move your derrière!

Adrián Berenguer-Beyond

High Vibrations

Disclaimer:

The use of psilocybin mushrooms, commonly known as magic mushrooms, carries potential risks and should be approached with caution. Psilocybin is a psychedelic compound that can induce altered states of consciousness and profound perceptual changes. It is important to note the following:

1. **Legal Considerations:** The cultivation, possession, and consumption of psilocybin-containing mushrooms are illegal in many jurisdictions. Before considering their use, individuals should be aware of and adhere to the laws of their respective locations.

2. **Health and Safety:** Psilocybin mushrooms can impact individuals differently, and the effects may be unpredictable. Individuals with a history of mental health issues, such as psychosis or schizophrenia, should avoid using psilocybin, as it may exacerbate or trigger underlying conditions.

3. **Pre-existing Conditions:** People with certain medical conditions, such as heart problems or a history of seizures, should consult with a healthcare professional before using psilocybin mushrooms, as the psychedelic effects can potentially affect these conditions.

4. **Interactions with Medications:** Psilocybin may interact with certain medications, including antidepressants and antipsychotics. It is crucial for individuals taking medications to consult with a healthcare provider to assess potential interactions.

5. **Pregnancy and Breastfeeding:** The effects of psilocybin on pregnancy and breastfeeding are not well-studied. Pregnant or breastfeeding individuals should avoid using psilocybin mushrooms due to potential risks to the developing fetus or nursing infant.

6. **Environmental Factors:** Set and setting play a significant role in the psychedelic experience. Individuals should only consider using psilocybin mushrooms in a safe and controlled environment, preferably with a trusted and experienced guide or a supportive, sober friend.

7. **Personal Responsibility:** It is essential for individuals to take responsibility for their own well-being. Prior research and education about the potential effects, risks, and legal implications of psilocybin use are imperative.

8. **Legal and Ethical Use:** Any discussion about the use of psilocybin mushrooms is not an endorsement of illegal activities. Individuals should be aware of and comply with the laws and regulations in their area.

In summary, the use of psilocybin mushrooms should be approached with careful consideration, and individuals are strongly encouraged to seek guidance from healthcare professionals and adhere to legal and ethical standards. If in doubt, it is advisable to refrain from using psilocybin mushrooms.

Sneaky Peaks

No time to find the times
We're all dancing on links and limes.
Lemons have all the rage what is all of this crazy beautiful craze.
Curled up telephone lines.
Redline elegant drones dimes and taxi lines.
Hats a drift in puddle lines
Steaks, medium hair drakes amongst all the fakes queer cakes and elegant
drakes scotch with a drop of lime times not lost in time.
Drop of the line clocks the time

Eights sevens and nines

Sneaky Peaks

No time to find the times
We're all dancing on links and limes.
Lemons have all the rage what is all of this crazy beautiful craze.
Curled up telephone lines.
Redline elegant drones dimes and taxi lines.
Hats a drift in puddle lines
Steaks, medium hair drakes amongst all the fakes queer cakes and elegant
drakes scotch with a drop of lime times not lost in time.
Drop of the line clocks the time

Eights sevens and nines

Soft Wild Highs ...

The soft, wild highs of life are the feelings of a soul full of wonder—like a hand out of the window, riding the airwaves, passing by fields of wheat and lavender. Fresh air fills the senses, calming yet imbued with a tender warmth, its confidence drawn from a ray of sunshine and the rasp of a smoky singer-songwriter. The highs and lows of a tone bouncing along the airwaves accompany you as you cruise down one-lane highways and open fields.

To enter a new way of thinking and being is what a soft, wild high feels like. An openness arises; in silence, one finds space. A creation-level event stirs the soul, leaving you with the feeling that you can accomplish anything with a sense of ease—no tension, just breath. There's a slight edge, like the sensation of a blade gliding across a sharpening stone. Soft, wild highs rejuvenate the spirit, evoking the energy of teenage years, excited about the path ahead.

A soft, wild high is like the roll of a ballpoint pen on a pad of paper—the pen glides, ink flows, and words ignite the page. It's a feeling we should all chase in life: a slight elevation in mood, just enough to see the beauty around us while maintaining a sharp train of thought. It's like the buzz of a bee flying past your ear—tingling the senses, awakening you with a fleeting moment of fright that quickly dissolves into calm.

Leaves crunch beneath your feet on a fall path, with tornado-like swirls of fallen debris—a soft, wild high.

Birds chirp in the breeze of a summer morning, a faint buzz of life mingling with a rooster's crow—a soft, wild high.

Lightning strikes as thunder rolls, the sky streaked with purples, grays, and blacks. Smears of light flash across a canvas of stormy clouds. As the storm passes, echoes crash over the land, leaving all who witness it with a daunting yet astounding feeling—a soft, wild high.

Flower gardens bloom with roses and daffodils, light gleaming, ladybugs and dragonflies flitting about. Scents fill the air, lifting spirits—a soft, wild high.

Rocks clink in a glass, a smooth spirit pours, a leather armchair invites. The first sip brings calmness that erupts within—a smooth, wild high.

These are just a few of the soft, wild highs of life. It's in the small moments that we come to appreciate what a wonderful life it is. Notice all the tiny details—the light filtering through the trees, painting intricate patterns on the ground—and watch as the larger picture broadens. This is where you'll find the gratitude that will lift your life into a soft, wild high.